"Diabetes? Wow..."

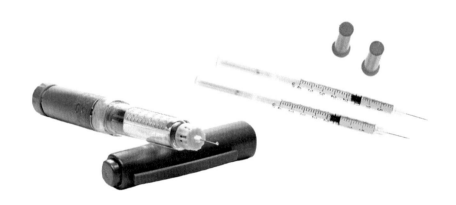

By

Briar Hoper

Author's note

When my son was diagnosed with Type 1 diabetes, I felt so overwhelmed by all the information I had to learn in a short time. I wanted to give my son a simpler introduction to all the things he would soon need to know. So I thought we would just go order a book for him. There must be thousands of them out there, right? Well, maybe not. There seemed to be any number of books with LOTS of pages full of words. But what thirteen-year-old wants to be presented with that book? And there are some great diabetes storybooks for children. I would have feared for my life if I tried to read one of those to my teenager. But that perfect book with lots of pictures and lots of information, but not TOO much information, seemed elusive. With time on my hands ... thanks to COVID-19 ... I decided to solve my own dilemma. I hope this book eases the transition for you and your loved ones.

Disclaimer

Contents

"Diabetes? Wow..."

What is Diabetes?

It isn't just one thing.

There are actually two main types of diabetes: **Type 1** and **Type 2**. Each type is its own disorder, not a different version or severity of the same disease. And yes, a person can have both at the same time.

Type 1

Type 1 diabetes (T1D) is an autoimmune disorder. The body's own immune system attacks the insulin-producing beta cells in the pancreas. Once these cells are gone, the body cannot produce its own insulin and will need insulin multiple times a day via injections or an insulin pump.

ISLETS OF LANGERHANS

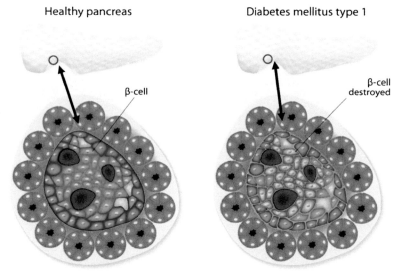

Healthy pancreas   Diabetes mellitus type 1

β-cell   β-cell destroyed

The Honeymoon Phase

A newly diagnosed person with diabetes will often experience a **honeymoon phase**. Before the body has destroyed all of the beta cells, it is still able to produce some insulin. This phase may last several months to a year or longer.

6

Type 2

Type 2 diabetes (T2D) is a disorder in which the body is not able to use the insulin it produces. People with Type 2 diabetes may be able to control their bodies' needs with diet and exercise, or may need to take medication and insulin.

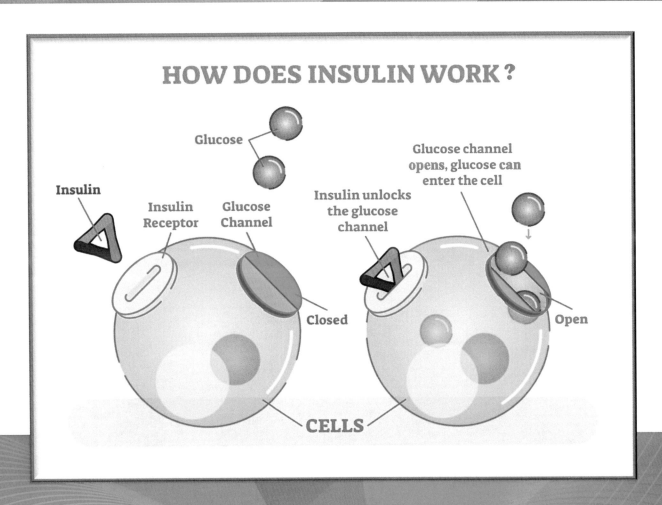

Insulin

Insulin is important to all parts of the body. The brain and muscles need glucose, a form of sugar, to function. Our body takes the food we eat and processes it into glucose (and some other things) to be used in the body for energy. Insulin is a hormone the cells need in order to use the glucose. Think of the insulin as a key that opens the door into the cell for glucose to enter. Without insulin, the glucose remains in the blood. Increased levels of glucose in the blood are harmful to the body, while at the same time the cells are starving.

Type 1 Diabetes: Signs and Symptoms

Excessive Thirst and Frequent Urination

Excessive thirst and increased urination are common Type 1 diabetes signs and symptoms. Excess glucose builds up in the blood. The kidneys are forced to work overtime to filter and absorb the excess glucose.

When the kidneys can't keep up, the excess glucose is excreted in urine, dragging along fluids from body tissues, which causes dehydration. This will usually leave a person with diabetes feeling thirsty. As they drink more fluids to quench their thirst, they'll urinate even more.

Extreme Fatigue, Hunger and Weight Loss

Type 1 diabetes can cause fatigue. Even though there may be lots of glucose available in the blood, without insulin the cells cannot access that fuel. The muscles fatigue easily. The lack of fuel reaching the body leads to constant hunger, and can potentially cause rapid weight loss.

Pain, Numbness and Tingling

Type 1 diabetics with prolonged high blood sugar can experience nerve damage called diabetic neuropathy. Neuropathy can result in pain, tingling and numbness. Numbness makes injuries harder to feel.

Blurred Vision

Blurred vision may be a sign glucose level is either too high or too low. The reason sight blurs may be fluid leaking into the lens of the eye. This makes the lens swell and change shape, so things start to look fuzzy.
(This also can happen when starting insulin due to shifting fluids, but it generally resolves after a few weeks.)

Unhealed Wound

Type 1 diabetes can impair wound healing. This can lead to infection and other complications. The feet are especially susceptible.

Urine Attracting Ants

Way back in history, before blood tests were possible, diabetes was sometimes diagnosed by the fact that ants were attracted to the excess sugar in the urine of a person with diabetes.

Is it contagious?

Exact causes are not known but it cannot be passed from person to person.

A person with Type 1 did not do anything to cause their diabetes and there is no known way to prevent it.

How did you get it?

Some Type 1 causes

Autoimmune

The body's own immune system mistakenly destroys the insulin-producing cells of the pancreas.

Family History

A family history increases the chance of developing Type 1 diabetes.

Environmental Factors

Exposure to viruses and other environmental influences may play a role in triggering the immune response.

Do you have to get shots?

MAYBE

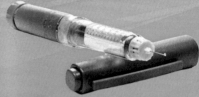

People with Type 1 diabetes cannot make their own insulin. They need to take insulin multiple times per day. This can be done with multiple daily injections (shots) or with an insulin pump.

What can you eat?

People with **Type 1** diabetes need to balance their food intake to their insulin dose (or their insulin dose to their food intake.) Like balancing a scale, the food and insulin effect must equal each other. A dietitian usually helps set up a plan for how to match insulin to food.

Carbohydrates are important as they are the main source of glucose. Fats, proteins and fiber digest much slower and have much less effect on blood glucose levels.

Chocolate Chip Cookies Nutrition Facts	
Servings: 24	
Amount per serving	
Calories	**260**
	% Daily Value*
Total Fat 12.3g	16%
Saturated Fat 7.9g	40%
Cholesterol 37mg	12%
Sodium 73mg	3%
Total Carbohydrate 34.7g	13%
Dietary Fiber 0.9g	3%
Total Sugars 21.5g	
Protein 3.2g	
Vitamin D 7mcg	33%
Calcium 47mg	4%
Iron 1mg	7%
Potassium 106mg	2%

*The % Daily Value (DV) tells you how much a nutrient in a food serving contributes to a daily diet. 2,000 calorie a day is used for general nutrition advice.

Counting carbohydrates is a common technique. A ratio of insulin to "carbs" is calculated for each **PWD** (person with diabetes). PWDs eat the food they choose and take the correct amount of insulin to match.

The **Constant Carbohydrate** plan uses a fixed dose of insulin at each meal and the same amount of carbohydrates each time.

The **Exchange Meal Plan** will include a set serving from six groups—starch, fruit, milk, fat, vegetable, and meat—at each meal.

THE PIZZA EFFECT

FOR THOSE ON INSULIN, SOME FOODS MAY BE PROBLEMATIC. FOODS THAT ARE HIGH IN FAT AND PROTEIN, LIKE PIZZA, CAN CAUSE A DELAYED RISE IN BLOOD GLUCOSE BECAUSE THE FAT AND PROTEIN SLOW THE DIGESTION OF CARBOHYDRATES. IF INSULIN IS DELIVERED AT THE USUAL TIME, IT MAY GET AHEAD OF DIGESTION AND CAUSE A LOW BLOOD SUGAR EVENT.

Every day a person with Type 1 diabetes must check their blood glucose frequently.

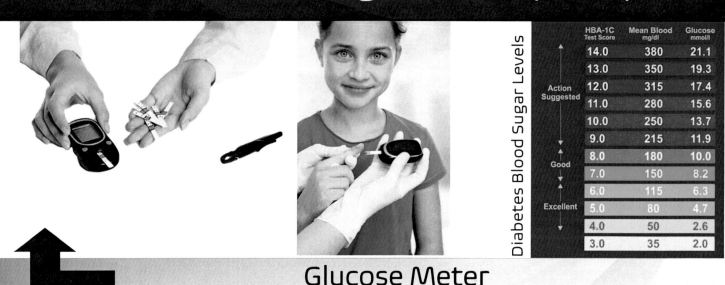

	HBA-1C Test Score	Mean Blood mg/dl	Glucose mmol/l
	14.0	380	21.1
	13.0	350	19.3
Action Suggested	12.0	315	17.4
	11.0	280	15.6
	10.0	250	13.7
	9.0	215	11.9
	8.0	180	10.0
Good	7.0	150	8.2
	6.0	115	6.3
Excellent	5.0	80	4.7
	4.0	50	2.6
	3.0	35	2.0

Diabetes Blood Sugar Levels

Glucose Meter

Blood glucose levels can be checked with a glucose meter. A lancing device is used to poke a finger. A test strip inserted in the meter is used to collect a small drop of blood. The meter will read the glucose level in the blood. This gives an immediate and accurate reading.

Continuous Glucose Monitor

Blood glucose levels can be checked with a continuous glucose monitor (CGM) .This device has a sensor which is inserted under the skin. A signal is sent every few minutes to a receiver or smartphone then maybe to a smart watch. CGMs gauge **interstitial fluid** so readings may lag 5-20 minutes behind a glucose meter.

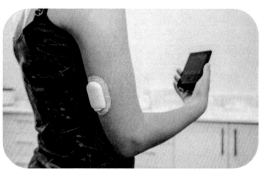

CGM and phone or receiver

Smartwatch with CGM Data

Every day a person with Type 1 diabetes must take insulin.

Disposable syringes use insulin from a vial for each dose.

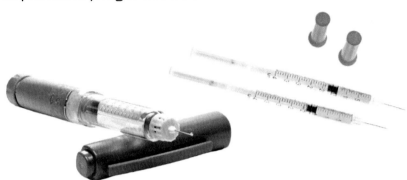

Insulin pens hold enough insulin for a number of days.

Multiple Daily Injections

Insulin is injected using a small needle. Two types of insulin are used in this method. A long acting insulin is injected to control the body's **basal** glucose production. A faster acting insulin is injected at meal time to **cover**, or balance, the glucose from food.

Insulin Pump

A popular option is to have a pump deliver insulin. An **infusion set** is inserted under the skin for several days. Only one type of insulin is used in the pump. A small amount is delivered continuously to control the body's basal glucose production. A **bolus** dose is delivered at meal time to cover, or balance, the glucose from food.

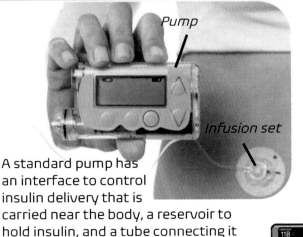

Pump

Infusion set

A standard pump has an interface to control insulin delivery that is carried near the body, a reservoir to hold insulin, and a tube connecting it to the infusion set which is changed every few days.

Tandem t:slim X2™ Insulin Pump

Omnipod DASH®

The Medtronic MiniMed™ 670G

A tubeless pump has a pump with a reservoir that is attached to the body for several days. It is connected via Bluetooth to a pump controller to program basal insulin delivery and bolus for food.

New technologies
make it easier

Artificial Pancreas & Closed Loop

Technology gets closer every year to mimicking the function of the pancreas. Some current and upcoming insulin pumps are able to function in connection with a continuous glucose monitor (CGM) to adjust insulin rates without active input from the person with diabetes (PWD). If the blood glucose is trending high, it will deliver more insulin. If the blood glucose is trending low, it will suspend insulin. A bolus for food must still be entered manually.

Tandem t:slim X2™ Insulin Pump with Control-IQ™ (Current)

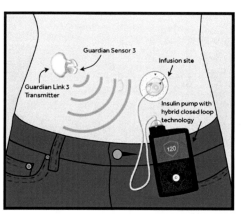

The Medtronic MiniMed™ 670G System (Current)
The Medtronic MiniMed™ 780G System (Upcoming)

Omnipod® 5 (Upcoming)

#WeAreNotWaiting

Frustrated with waiting for pharmaceutical companies and FDA approval, a grassroots group of T1Ds and parents of T1Ds formed this group to create technologies on their own. #WeAreNot Waiting was responsible for making CGM data available through the cloud and the first DIY closed loop systems. It continues to push innovation to the next level.

Tidepool Loop

Building from the #WeAreNotWaiting projects, Tidepool Loop will be an FDA-approved phone app that integrates current CGMs and insulin pumps to create a closed loop system.

Tidepool Project © 2020

Can you die from it?

YES

... although with good management the chances are greatly reduced.

The risks

- Hypoglycemic coma
- Diabetic ketoacidosis
- Complications of long term poor blood sugar control

Hypoglycemic unawareness

Some people may not feel the signs of low blood sugar. This makes them more likely to go into a hypoglycemic coma.

Healthy practices

- Maintain blood sugar levels
- Make those around a person with T1D aware in case of emergency
- Stay active
- Seek mental health support
- See endocrinologist regularly

Medical alert ID

Medical alert ID will make responders aware of possible reasons for symptoms and let them know to treat diabetes if the person is unconscious or injured for other reasons.

A Short History of Diabetes

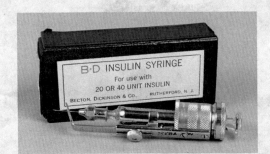

Diabetes was first recorded in 1552 B.C. in Egypt. It was recognized throughout history as a disease of excessive urine or sugar urine. Patients with diabetes were not given long to live ... until the discovery of insulin. It wasn't until 1922 that Fredrick Banting and his team figured out how to effectively treat patients with insulin. They received the Nobel Prize. Since that early breakthrough, treatment has advanced an incredible amount. Early treatment was done with a reusable syringe that had to be boiled for each use. Glucose levels were checked in the urine. Today there are continuous glucose monitors (CGMs) to check blood glucose every five minutes, and numerous ways to administer insulin.

Do you need

ONE OF THE THINGS MOST PEOPLE <u>DO</u> KNOW IS THAT A PERSON WITH Type 1 DIABETES MAY NEED TO EAT A SUGARY SNACK.

Low Blood Sugar (Hypoglycemia)

When a person with diabetes does not have enough glucose in their blood the body and brain cannot function. **Hypoglycemia** can be caused by using up the glucose with activity or by taking more insulin than is needed. Usually the problem is solved with a small amount of sugary food or drink to quickly bring the blood sugar back to normal

Glucose Tablets

Fruit Juice

Regular Soda

Skittles, etc

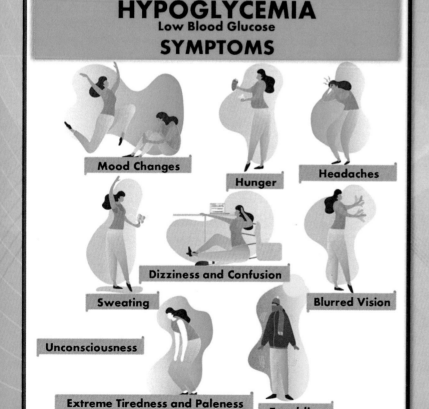

Hypoglycemic coma

Severely low blood glucose can cause unconsciousness and even death. A severe hypoglycemic event is a true emergency. A person with diabetes should carry emergency glucagon treatment. This can be injected like insulin or placed as a powder in the nostril.

What is glucagon?

Glucagon is a hormone also produced in the pancreas. Glucagon tells the liver to release glucose into the blood stream.

16

HIGH BLOOD GLUCOSE CAN BE A PROBLEM TOO.

High Blood Sugar (Hyperglycemia)

When a person with diabetes does not have enough insulin in their body, the glucose remains in the blood. This is called **hyperglycemia**. This is what causes many of the symptoms by which diabetes can be recognized.

Ketones

Ketones are chemicals the liver makes when it can't get energy from glucose. The body needs another source, so it uses fat. The liver turns fat into ketones, a type of acid. In small amounts, ketones are normal, but in T1D they can build up in the blood.

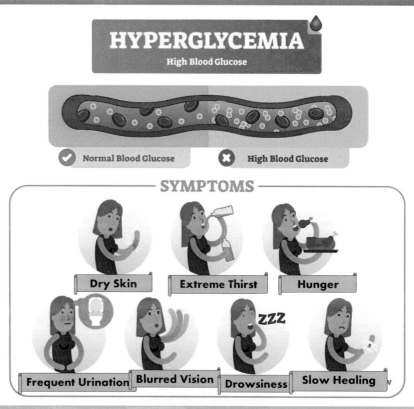

HYPERGLYCEMIA
High Blood Glucose

✓ Normal Blood Glucose   ✕ High Blood Glucose

— SYMPTOMS —

Dry Skin | Extreme Thirst | Hunger

Frequent Urination | Blurred Vision | Drowsiness | Slow Healing

DKA

Diabetic ketoacidosis (DKA) is a serious condition that can lead to **diabetic coma** (passing out for a long time) or even death. High levels of ketones can poison the body. When levels get too high it can cause DKA. Treatment for DKA usually happens in a hospital.

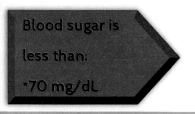

Blood sugar is less than: *70 mg/dL

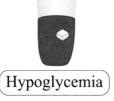

Hypoglycemia

Norm

Hyperglycemia

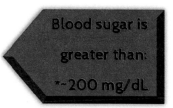

Blood sugar is greater than: *~200 mg/dL

*Each physician may have unique recommendation for ranges depending on age or other factors.

Complications?

Eyeballs & KIDNEYS & Nerves OH MY!

The leading causes of death for Type 1 diabetics stem from complications of poorly maintained blood sugar. Long periods of high blood sugar cause damage to many organs in the body.

Diabetes Complications

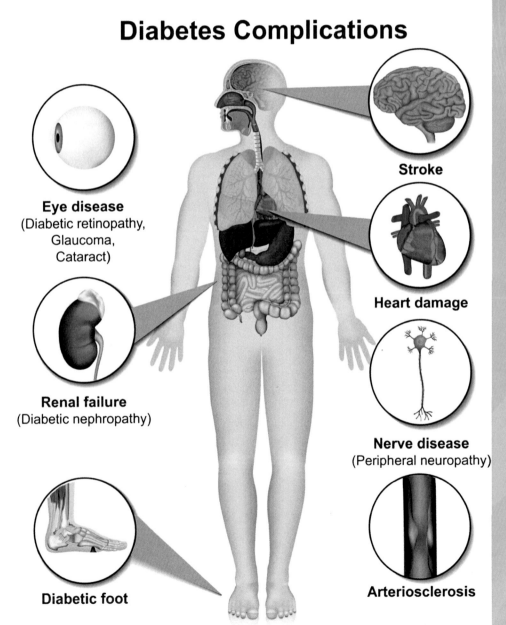

Stroke

Eye disease
(Diabetic retinopathy, Glaucoma, Cataract)

Heart damage

Renal failure
(Diabetic nephropathy)

Nerve disease
(Peripheral neuropathy)

Diabetic foot

Arteriosclerosis

HbA1c

A good indicator of health and blood glucose control is a person's HbA1c (A1c) level. An **A1c test** measures the amount of blood sugar attached to hemoglobin. It is a standard part of diagnosing diabetes and is checked frequently to make sure levels stay within a safe range. **Hemoglobin** is a protein found in blood. When glucose builds up in the blood, it binds to the hemoglobin. Blood cells live for about three months. By testing how much glucose is bound to the hemoglobin in a person's blood, doctors get an idea of how high the average blood glucose was during those three months.

Will it go away?

NO

Diabetes has no cure (yet). Researchers are working hard to develop a cure for diabetes.

Anxiety & Depression

It is common for people with diabetes to feel anxious or depressed following diagnosis. The support of friends and family is important at this time.

Help is available

Most people with diabetes will seek help at some point in their life. Anxiety, depression and burnout are all good reasons to seek help. An endocrinologist can recommend someone who specializes in understanding diabetes and mental health.

Diabetes Burnout

Diabetes burnout is when someone with diabetes gets tired of managing their condition, and ignores it for a time. Living with diabetes can be overwhelming and it is not unusual to feel burned out.

Some symptoms of diabetes burnout

- Strong negative feelings about diabetes.
- Feeling controlled by diabetes.
- Feeling alone with diabetes care.
- Avoiding some, or all, diabetes management.
- Feeling unmotivated to change habits.

What about school?

People with diabetes have to treat their diabetes every day.

School is no exception.

504 School Health Plan

Under section 504 of the Rehabilitation Act, any student with special health needs can make a **504 plan** with the school for how those needs will be met at school. An endocrinologist can help get the needed medical requirements. Parents, students and a school nurse or other representative will meet to hammer out the details to ensure that the student's medical needs are met and their rights protected.

ADA & ADA

The **American Diabetes Association (ADA)** has many resources for diabetics.

The **Americans with Disabilities Act (ADA)** follows on the heels of the 504 Rehabilitation act, and contains provisions to protect the rights of people with diabetes. Children with diabetes cannot be excluded from school and activities due to diabetes, and they have the right to receive help caring for diabetes during school.

Can you still play sports?

YES

NOT ONLY ARE PEOPLE WITH DIABETES ABLE TO PLAY SPORTS, EXERCISE IS RECOMMENDED.

Jordan Morris, Seattle Sounders

Saley, 15 , California

Danny, 16, Michigan

Danny, 15, Michigan

Exercise:

- Increases insulin sensitivity (insulin works better)
- Lowers blood sugar levels
- Increases energy and endurance throughout the day
- Increases muscle tone
- Makes for a healthier heart and lower blood pressure
- Promotes better sleep at night
- Increases resistance to illness
- Lowers stress, anxiety, boredom, frustration and depression

Braxton, 13, Texas

Professional Athletes with T1D

Lauren Cox: WNBA

Jay Cutler: NFL, Denver Broncos

Kris Freeman: Olympic skier, USA

Sara Groenewegen: Softball, Canada

Mark Lowe: MLB, Detroit Tigers

Kristina Tomić: Flyweight, Croatia

And many more ...

Adrenaline

While exercise generally decreases blood sugar, sometimes—especially with extreme or competitive sports—**adrenaline** can cause a rise in blood sugar. This may later be followed by low blood sugar. Adrenaline is a hormone released by the adrenal gland .This is what causes the "fight or flight" reaction. Glucose is released to fuel the brain. Other situations that cause an adrenaline release may include: injury, surprise (like seeing a spider), stress (such as the first day of school) and excitement (like playing video games).

Do you feel sick?

NOT USUALLY

PEOPLE WHOSE BLOOD GLUCOSE IS UNDER CONTROL USUALLY ENJOY THE SAME LEVEL OF HEALTH AS ANYONE ELSE.

Sick Days

Having a cold, flu or other illness can make diabetes harder to control. Hormones released by the body to combat illness can cause blood glucose to rise. The body releases extra ketones when fighting an illness. People with diabetes need to take extra care when sick to stay hydrated and continue to take medication and insulin. More insulin than normal may be needed.

T1D and other autoimmune disorders

People with Type 1 diabetes, an **autoimmune disorder**, are more likely than non T1Ds to develop other autoimmune disorders. The reason is not understood, although genetics likely plays a role.

Some co-occurring autoimmune disorders:

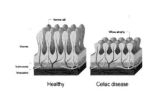

CELIAC DISEASE

Celiac Disease

The body attacks the small intestine. A gluten-free diet will alleviate symptoms.

Healthy   Celiac disease

Thyroid disease

The body attacks the thyroid gland, leading to too much or too little thyroid hormone. Pills and sometimes radiation or thyroid removal are used as treatment.

THYROID DISEASE

Also: Gastritis, Addison's Disease, Vitiligo

How is your family?

Siblings

- May worry about their loved one's health.
- May also worry about whether they will develop diabetes.
- May feel neglected due to attention their sibling is receiving.
- May resent changes in family life or diet.

Diabetes sucks

Parents

- May feel guilt that they didn't notice sooner, couldn't prevent it, etc.
- May feel overwhelmed with learning to care for their child, or helpless if their child is an adult.
- May grieve over the diagnosis.
- May feel anger.
- May fear for their child's future.

I wish it was me instead.

Friends

I don't know what to do.

- May feel unsure how to talk to their friend.
- May resent friend's inability to eat any time, anywhere.
- May put pressure on their friend to behave as they did before diagnosis.
- May feel overprotective.

Too much information!

Grandparents

- May feel sad for their grandchild.
- May feel overwhelmed with information.
- May resent or not understand why they are not allowed to care for their grandchild.
- May make their usual tasty treats, which their grandchild can no longer eat without taking insulin.

I've never met
MANY PEOPLE HAVEN'T

PEOPLE WITH DIABETES ARE JUST LIKE ANYONE ELSE. MANY PEOPLE MAY KNOW SOMEONE WITH DIABETES AND NEVER KNEW THEY HAD IT.

Madison, 15, Florida

Walker, 15, Georgia

Jack, 6, Ohio

Izzy, 10, Colorado

Hannah, 11, North Carolina

anyone with T1D.

Carson, 15, Indiana

Jacob, 7, Florida

Johanna, 3, Ohio

Kaden, 10, Pennsylvania

Claetyn, 13, Texas

Emily, 10, Delaware

Ophelia, 2, Ohio

"Diaversary"

Many people recognize the anniversary of their diagnosis in some way. It is a celebration of the strength of character it takes to overcome and thrive with diabetes.

25

Diabetes abbreviations/acronyms

A1c ....Glycerated Hemoglobin

ADA..American Diabetes Association

ADA..Americans with Disabilities Act

BG..Blood Glucose

BS..Blood Sugar

CGM...Continuous Glucose Monitor

DKA..Diabetic Ketoacidosis

DM..Diabetes Mellitus

Endo...Endocrinologist (Diabetes Dr.)

GM...Glucose Meter

HbA1c (A1c)..Glycerated Hemoglobin

LADA...Latent Autoimmune Diabetes in Adults

MDI..Multiple Daily Injections

Mg/dL..Milligrams per deciliter

Mmol/L..Millimoles per liter

PWD..Person/People with diabetes

T1D...Type 1 diabetes /diabetic

T2D...Type 2 diabetes /diabetic

Glossary

504 Plan...Plan for healthcare needs at school

Adrenaline..Hormone that triggers "fight or flight"

Alpha cells..Cells that secrete glucagon

Arteriosclerosis..Hardening of the arteries

Autoantibodies...Antibodies that attack the body's own cells

Autoimmune disorder....................................The body's own immune system attacks

Basal insulin/rate...In T1D, the small amount of insulin kept
constant by MDI/pump

Beta cells..Cells in the pancreas that secrete insulin

Bolus...The insulin taken to cover food

Glossary—continued

Carbohydrate............Main source of fuel for the body, broken down into glucose

Constant carbohydrate plan..........Diet plan with fixed doses of insulin and carbs

Counting carbohydrates......................Diet plan of matching insulin dose to carbs

Cover (carbohydrates)...............Taking the correct dose of insulin to match carbs

Dawn phenomenon..Early morning rise in blood sugar

Diabetic coma................................Unconsciousness due to high or low blood sugar

Diabetic ketoacidosis...Ketones build up to dangerous levels

Diabetes mellitus..............................Diabetes characterized by the body's inability
to use blood sugar properly, includes T1 and T2

Exchange meal plan...........Diet plan with set dose of insulin and choices from six
food groups

Glucagon...Hormone that tells the liver to release glucose

Hemoglobin..Protein that carries oxygen in the blood

Honeymoon phase...........................Period when pancreas still makes some insulin

Hyperglycemia..High blood sugar

Hypoglycemia..Low blood sugar

Hypoglycemic unawareness...................A person does not feel the symptoms of
low blood sugar

Infusion set...Connects an insulin pump to the body

Insulin..Hormone that allows glucose to enter cells

Insulin resistance..................................When cells do not respond well to insulin

Interstitial Fluid...Fluid that surrounds the body's cells

Ketones..Byproduct of turning fat into energy

Lipohypertrophy...An injection site cannot absorb
insulin properly due to overuse

Nephropathy...Kidney damage

Neuropathy..Nerve damage

Pancreas...Organ that makes insulin and glucagon

Retinopathy...Damage to the retina of the eye

Stroke..................Blood supply to brain is interrupted due to damage or blockage

Target range..Goal range for blood sugar in diabetics

About the Author

Briar Hoper is a dance instructor in a small town in Washington where she lives with her husband and two sons. Briar graduated from Eastern Washington University and is a singer, dancer, actor, choreographer and writer in the local theater scene. This is her first published work.

Photo credits

Pg. 13, Pg. 14, Medtronic: Medtronic.com; Pg. 13, Omnipod, Omnipod wearer; Pg. 14, Omnipod 5: Insulet Corporation; Pg. 13, Pg. 14, Tandem: Tandem Diabetes Care, Inc.; Pg. 14, bottom right: Tidepool Project © 2020; Pg. 15, Medical ID: Briar Hoper; Pg. 15, bottom: Division of Medicine and Science, National Museum of American History, Smithsonian Institution; Pg. 16, Glucagon kit: Briar Hoper; Pg. 21, Jordan Morris: Mike Fiechtner Photography; Pg. 21: Teresa Asch, Stacie Stokes, Shea Sawyer; Pg. 24: Nikki Bellotte, Matthew A. Graham, Olga Siler, Sheri Mackzum, Kimber Jones; Pg. 25: Stacy Mundy Photography, Desiree Palmer, Liz Rusche, Jayme Crocker, Ashton Moore, Elizabeth Reetz, Brenda Gibbner

With the exception of the above, all photographs and artwork in this book are credited to depositphotos.com.

References

American Diabetes Association. 1995-2020. 16 August 2020 (diabetes.org)

Beyond Type 1. 16 August 2020 (beyondtype1.org)

Diabetes Self Management. 2020. 16 August 2020 (diabetesselfmanagement.com)

Empower. 16 August 2020. (empoweryourhealth.org)

Everyday Health. 1996-2020. 16 August 2020. (everydayhealth.com)

Geisinger. 2020. 16 August 2020. (geisinger.org)

Healthline. 2005-2020. 16 August 2020 (healthline.com)

Insulin Nation. 2020. 16 August 2020 (insulinnation.com)

Jordan Morris Foundation. 2020. (jordanmorrisfoundation.com)

Kids Health from Nemours. 1995-2020. 16 August 2020 (kidshealth.org)

Lilly. 2018. 16 August 2020 (lillyglucagon.com)

Lilly USA. 16 August 2020 (baqsimi.com)

Mayo Clinic. 1998-2020. 16 August 2020 (mayoclinic.org)

MedecineNet. 1996-2020. 16 August 2020 (medecinenet.com)

MySugar. 16 August 2020. (mysugr.com)

National Institute of Diabetes and Digestive and Kidney Diseases. 16 August 2020. (niddk.nih.gov)

Nightscout #We Are Not Waiting. 2020. 16 August 2020 (nightscout.info)

Remedy Health Media. 2020. 16 August 2020. (endocrineweb.com)

Tandem Diabetes Care, Inc. 2020. 16 August 2020 (tandemdiabetes.com)

Tidepool Project © 2020. 16 August 2020 (tidepool.org)

TriHealth. 2020 Trihealth. 16 August 2020 (trihealth.com)

WebMD. 2005-2020. 16 August 2020 (webmd.com)

Made in United States
North Haven, CT
29 August 2023

40886568R00018